# 150 Proven Ways to Make Money Online in 2019 – And the Secrets to Success

## *The Most Comprehensive List In the World*

by James Pratterson

# Prologue

**Warning:** This book will give you **too many** ideas.

Wondering how to make money online? Or perhaps you've already tried, but haven't had any success?

Well, you've come to the right place.

To my knowledge, **this is the most comprehensive list in the world of secrets to making money online.** These are the current methods that have been proven to work in 2019. Because every legitimate online earning method is included, there's a huge range in income potential – some methods can make you a millionaire (if you put in the work), while others are only good for pocket change.

Whether you're looking to make a full-time income working from home or simply want to find a good side hustle, I'm sure you'll have tons of ideas by the end.

As you'll see, income potential is included for most of the methods of making money, which is on a scale of 1-5 [1 being the lowest income potential, 5 being the highest (millions +)].

In many cases the income potential is virtually impossible to give (such as in the case of online investing), so consider the potential scale to be a general guideline.

Without further ado, here's the list!

# Table of Contents

# 1. Affiliate Marketing

Ever wondered how some people make thousands of dollars every month online?

More likely than not, it's from **affiliate marketing**.

Affiliate marketing is so lucrative that even major media sites like the New York Times are **adding affiliate sites** to their portfolios.

The age of banner ads is waning, while affiliate marketing has only grown over the years.

**But what exactly IS affiliate marketing?**

It works like this:

You can promote any product with a special "affiliate link". When someone clicks that link and purchases a product, you get paid a portion of the sale price (at no expense to the buyer).

In other words, **you can sell anything online without even owning it!**

Although you'll only get a small percentage of the sale, it adds up fast and many affiliate marketers make tens, or even **hundreds of thousands of dollars per month**. Granted, it does take a lot of time to reach that level…anywhere from a year to several years, depending on how much work you put into it.

But the end results speak for themselves.

Though it will definitely take some work, affiliate marketing is actually very easy. You don't need any inventory, it's not a hassle like drop-shipping, and it can be done using only a computer and a Wi-Fi connection.

For these reasons, **affiliate marketing is my number one recommendation for making money online**.
For those of you who are interested, I know of some awesome training which covers every aspect of affiliate marketing, and makes it very easy for beginners to understand and get started.

In fact, it's the exact training that got me started!

**Secret to Success:**

Use Amazon Associates as it is the most successful affiliate program in the world, by a wide margin.

**Income potential: 5/5**

## 2. Get Paid to Take Surveys

Do you enjoy filling out surveys?

I know, that's probably a silly question…. But what if you could get paid to fill out surveys? Would you enjoy it then? Well, there's some good news:

**Many websites PAY you to take surveys**. The earnings aren't all that great, as most surveys sites only pay a dollar or two per hour. Still, some people make thousands of dollars every year using this method.

Surveys can be frustrating, however, since they take a long time to complete and the pay is well below minimum wage in the US. But if you do it mindlessly while watching TV, you'll turn wasteful hours into cash!

**Secret to Success:**

Perhaps the most famous survey site is **Swagbucks**. There are many surveys available on Swagbucks at any given moment, and the pay is about as good as it gets.

If you don't like Swagbucks, there are plenty of other options. Here's a few to get you started:

- **SurveyJunkie**

- **Harris Poll Online**
- **Global Test Market**
- **E-Poll Surveys**
- **PineCone Research**
- **YouGov**
- **OneOpinion**
- **Fusion Cash**
- **Vindale Research**
- **VIPVoice**
- **PaidViewPoint**

**Income potential: 2/5**

# 3. Install These Apps on Your Phone

How'd you like to earn some completely passive income?

There are several apps you can download on your phone which will track your phone use. In exchange for this…well, intrusion, you'll get paid!

If you don't mind a research company tracking everything you do on your phone, then by all means download these apps!

**It doesn't take any work on your part, but you can make a little extra spending money every month.**

**Secret to Success:**

Here are the most reputable ones:

1. **MobileXpression**– Free $5 gift card after one week *(keep app installed for 30 days)
2. **ShopTracker** – Free $3 gift card for signing up
3. **Nielson Mobile Panel**

**Income potential: 1/5**

# 4. Get Paid to Complete Easy Tasks

"Get Paid To" or "GPT" websites pay you to complete certain tasks, such as taking surveys, completing offers, searching the internet, etc.

Although the money is easy to earn, it takes a lot of time and is far below minimum wage.

**Nonetheless, it is still a good way to add a few dollars to your wallet each month.**

**Secret to Success:**

Here's a list of the top GPT sites out there:

- **Swagbucks**
- **InboxDollars**
- **Earnhoney**
- **Fusion Cash**
- **InstaGC**
- **CashCrate**
- **Irazoo** (enter the code XAHJGH to earn bonus points when you join!)

- **PrizeRebel**
- **Points2Shop**
- **Earnably**
- **GrabPoints**
- **TreasureTrooper**
- **QuickRewards**
- **EarningStation**
- **SuperPay.me**
- **GrindaBuck**
- **KeepRewarding**
- **RewardingWays**
- **GiftHunterClub**
- **OfferNation**

Income potential: 2/5

## 5. Sell a Simple Service for $5 on Fiverr

You can sell pretty much anything on Fiverr.

A lot of people sell traditional services, or "gigs", such as ghostwriting, editing, **graphic design**, and web development.

Others sell more…unique…services. Such as singing happy birthday to anyone you desire, or making prank phone calls.

The possibilities are literally endless.

**Secret to Success:**

**The standard rate for a Fiverr gig is $5, but you can charge much more if you offer a valuable service.**
Sound like fun?

**Join Fiverr!**

**Income potential: 3/5**

# 6. Create and Sell Your Own Online Course

Do you have extensive knowledge in a particular subject? It can be anything – math, web design, bodybuilding, whatever.

As long as you know your field inside and out, why not create an online course to share your knowledge?

Depending on the topic, this can be an extremely lucrative way to make money online. **Some people make over $1 million per year!**

Creating a good online course takes a lot of time and hard work. It's not uncommon to work on a course for several months before launching it. But it's well worth the effort.

**Secret to Success:**

Speaking of launching it, there are several websites where you can sell your course. My favorite, and one that many people have had huge success with, is **Teachable**.

That said, here are some other options worth looking into:

- **Udemy**
- **Thinkific**

- Skillshare
- learnWorlds
- CourseCraft
- Ruzuku
- PathWright
- Kajabi
- DigitalChalk

**Income potential: 5/5**

# 7. Earn $0.10/Day to View Lockscreen Ads

Do you own a smartphone?

For virtually no work at all, you could be earning an extra **$36.50 per year!**

S'more is an app that pays you 10 cents a day to show an ad on your lockscreen, even if you never click any ads.

When you sign up, use this code to earn $0.25 instantly: **CJFNO9**

You can't redeem your earnings until you reach $1.50, so 25 cents will speed up the process by 2 days :).

You can also earn money for referrals, and for taking surveys.

**Secret to Success:**

**As a Bonus,** you can download other lock screen cash apps to earn even more from your phone! Check out these:

- Slidejoy – Lock Screen Cash
- Fronto Lock Screen
- Adme Rewards Locker
- LifeSlide – Lock Screen, Unlock Money
- Paid Unlock
- Unlock & Win! by Perk

**Income potential: 1/5**

# 8. Teach ESL to Foreign Students Online

Are you fluent in the English language? There's a lot of money to be had by teaching ESL to foreign students through online platforms.

Here are a couple of the best ones:

- **VipKid** – teach ESL to Chinese students
- **DadaABC** – teach ESL to Chinese students
- **iTalki** – teach any language online

The pay for these sites is generally in the **$10-20/hour range with benefits**. Also, some (not all) ESL sites require that you have teaching experience or at least a Bachelor's degree.

You can also set up your own website where you offer English lessons – this could potentially be more profitable, but it would also take a lot longer to get any clients.

**Secret to Success:**

In order to teach ESL online, you will need a video calling software. Skype and Google Hangouts are the most popular options. For slow connections, I have found that **Gruveo** works well.

Another requirement is a quality, **noise-canceling headset**.

**Income potential: 3/5**

# 9. Create YouTube Videos and Monetize them with Ads

Creating **YouTube** videos is definitely a good, tried-and-true approach to making money online. However, unless you have millions of people watching your videos, it won't make you rich.

If you monetize your videos with ads, **you can expect to earn roughly $2,000 per million views**.

**Secret to Success:**

**Affiliate marketing** is another way you can monetize your videos. For example, if you do product reviews, include an affiliate link to that product in your video description.

**Income potential: 5/5**

# 10.  Start an Amazon FBA Business Selling Private Label Products

Here's how selling private label products on Amazon works (in a tiny nutshell):

**You find a generic product on Amazon, add your own branding to it, and then resell it at a markup.**
If your product is in the top 100 bestsellers for your category, you can make thousands of dollars per day! However, a more typical income is in the $1,000-2,000/month range.

**Secret to Success:**

The most successful Amazon sellers pick very in-demand products and do extensive marketing. It can be very time-consuming, but if it makes you a millionaire, who cares?

**Income potential: 5/5**

# 11.  Build Smartphone Apps for Free, or Hire Someone Else to

The app industry is huge, yet still new enough that it's not oversaturated. This means huge opportunity for app developers!

**And believe it or not, you don't even have to know how to code to build an app.**

With **Appypie**, you can build apps without coding knowledge, and without paying a dime!

**Secret to Success:**

If you are serious about making apps and earning money from them, you will want to **hire a developer** though.

**Income potential: 5/5**

# 12.  Make Money from Your Livestreams with the Peeks App

Have you been doing your livestreams on Facebook or Periscope?

You may want to switch to a new app….

**Peeks is an ecommerce-enabled livestream app that allows people viewing your livestream to easily send you tips.**

**Secret to Success:**

If you become popular and build up a large following, you could make a killing every time you go live!

**Income potential: 2/5**

# 13.    Do Graphic Design

Graphic design is becoming a more and more important asset to online businesses in these days of visual appeal and user experience.

**If you are any good at graphic design, chances are you could land a paying job, and likely multiple paying jobs.**

Online businesses need to have good visuals and an appealing overall design if they are interested in truly succeeding.

Most online businesses turn to the tried and true methods of acquiring design talent by hiring designers off of platforms such as the following:

- **Upwork**
- **Fiverr**
- **Freelancer**
- **Envato Studio**
- **PeoplePerHour**

Therefore, as a graphic designer, these are the sites you'll want to focus on – especially in the beginning.

**Secret to Success:**

In order to get the highest-paying jobs, you'll have to make yourself stand out from the crowd. This isn't easy, but it's very necessary – it's what weeds out the great designers from the mediocre ones.

# 14.   Get Paid to Search on Google and other Large Websites

Want to get paid for searching on eBay, Amazon, and Google? Join **Qmee**!

When you have the Qmee browser extension installed, ads will show up on the side of your screen every so often. Each time you click one of these ads, you will earn a few cents.

**I've earned more than $68 so far on Qmee:**

Your Qmee history

Total earnings
$68.33

Total cash outs
$68.33

**Secret to Success:**

One of the great things about Qmee is that you aren't required to have a certain amount of earnings before you can cash out. That means you can install Qmee today, click just one ad, and immediately cash out your earnings!

You can also make money with referrals and surveys on Qmee.

**Income potential: 2/5**

# 15.   Make $200+ a Month Watching Videos

Getting paid to watch movies sounds too good to be true, right?

Believe it or not, there are many sites that pay you to do just that!

The pay is pretty terrible at just a couple cents per video, but there's a neat hack you can use to make the most in the shortest amount of time.

**Here's what to do:**

If you have any unused, outdated electronics sitting around, why not put them to work earning you money!?

Just set them up to auto-play the videos, and watch the pennies roll in!

Some people have reported earning $200+ per month with this method.

**Secret to Success:**

Both **Swagbucks** and **EarnHoney** work with this method.

**Income potential: 2/5**

# 16. Get Cash Back on Your Online Purchases

Do you shop online? If so, you might want to look into joining a cash-back website.

When you shop through them at a merchant like Amazon or Walmart, you'll earn a small percentage back for everything you buy!

Depending on the site, the percentage can range from 1-70+%, so as you can see it's really all over the place.

**Secret to Success:**

Here are the best cash back websites:

- **Ebates** (get $10 for free when you sign up)
- **MyPoints**
- **Shop at home**
- **BeFrugal**
- **MrRebates**
- **Extrabux**
- **Ibotta** (app)
- **Dosh** (app)

**Income potential: 2/5**

# 17.   Earn $30/Hour Testing Websites

Want to help webmasters build better websites?

Sites like **UserTesting** connect webmasters looking for an opinion on their sites to people who want to earn money for testing websites.

**Just film yourself critiquing a website for a certain length of time, send it in when you're done, and get paid!**

**Secret to Success:**

Freelance website testing can earn you well above minimum wage. But tests are not always available, and when they are people snatch them up pretty quickly. So if you want to make a living doing this, be sure to accept the offers right away.

Here are a few more website testing websites :

- **IntelliZoom**
- **WhatUsersDo**

- **TestingTime**
- **Userlytics**
- **UserTest**
- **TryMyUI**

**Income potential: 3/5**

# 18.   Get Rewarded for Staying Healthy

Everyone knows it's important to stay healthy…but few know it can help your bank account too! There are actually a number of health and fitness apps that pay you to stay healthy. Really!

**Achievement** is an app that actually pays you for staying healthy. It connects to more than 30 health, fitness, and lifestyle apps and rewards you points based on activities like walking, meditating, and logging food, and even…sleeping!
**Secret to Success:**

**Once you reach 10,000 points, you can redeem them for $10!**

Apparently, points can take a long time to earn, so don't expect to download the app and cash in your earnings by tomorrow.

Here are a few more apps and websites to check out if you want to get paid to stay healthy:

- **HealthyWage**
- **Sweatcoin**
- **StepBet**
- **DietBet**

**Income potential: 2/5**

# 19. Become a Freelance Writer

Think you're a decent writer?

Well, you're in luck because writing for the web is a very in-demand job these days, and it's just becoming more so in 2019.

If you're a native English speaker from the United States, all the better.

Most writing jobs pay peanuts (like $10 for 1,000 words), but if you have a powerful portfolio and a knack for producing engaging, high-quality content, you can expect a lot more.

True wordsmiths can make hundreds of dollars per article.

**Secret to Success:**

**How do you get started? You have a couple options:**
Go out on your own and search for clients on Facebook (there are writer's groups specifically for this) and other social media, or join a website like **Upwork** and bid on available writing jobs.

**Income potential: 4/5**

# 20.   Do Technical Freelancing

**If you're a techy person, you can utilize your skills to make a good living online.**

There's a wide range of angles you could take, including fixing WordPress errors, developing websites and apps, and – believe it or not – converting files from one type to another.

For larger, more involved tasks (like building an app), go with Upwork. When people post jobs, you can give them a bid and show them some examples of your work.

**Secret to Success:**

For quick tasks however, check out **Fiverr**. You can charge people $5 for a simple service, and offer extra upgrades for an additional cost.

**Income potential: 4/5**

# 21.　**Help People Get Things Done as a Virtual Assistant**

Assisting people with your professional services online is a great way to make an income.

Virtual Assistants (or VAs) help out with a variety of tasks, ranging from technical to creative. Obviously one VA can't do everything, so if you specify your strengths you'll be more likely to get hired.

**Secret to Success:**

In order to reach the largest number of potential employers, your best bet would be to **join Upwork, Indeed, or Remote.co.**

**Income potential: 3/5**

# 22.   Earn $20+/Hour to Tutor Students Online

Are you good with academics and great at teaching? Becoming a virtual tutor may be the right job for you.

As a virtual tutor, you'll be helping students with their school work. For a fee, that is.

Here's a list of great tutoring websites, many of which pay up to $20+/hour!

- **Chegg**
- **Tutor.com**
- **RevolutionPrep**
- **TutorVista**
- **Flexjobs tutor**
- **SmartThinking**
- **BrainFuse**
- **Skooli**
- **Tutorhub**

**Secret to Success:**

If you're the teacher-type, you may also enjoy **creating an online course** (plus, this can be far more profitable).

**Income potential: 3/5**

## 23. Join a Focus Group and Earn $50-$200+

By participating in an online focus group, you can earn some pretty decent cash.

Online focus groups are typically used for consumer research, business-to-business research and political research.

**Secret to Success:**

**It may sound boring, but you can make anything from $50-200+ for participating.** You should be aware that some focus groups can last several hours.

Here are a few companies to try:

- **ProOpinion**
- **MindSwarms**
- **FocusGroup**

**Income potential: 2/5**

# 24.   Use a Different Search Engine (Earn Up to $1 per Search)

Want to get paid for browsing the web? **There are many companies that pay you to use their search engine!**

In fact, **I once made $1 for just one web search!**

Getting paid to search is one of my favorite ways to make money online, because it's literally passive income. I'm getting paid for something I already do!

**Secret to Success:**

Here's a few tips you should keep in mind when using any paid to search platform:

- **Don't search fast.** If you do a bunch of random searches over a short period of time trying to get paid, you will most likely get caught. Usually, the consequence for this is getting paid less often.
- **Try to stay on the search results for 30+ seconds.** By staying on the search results page for at least 30 seconds, you'll appear legitimate and be a valued user.
- **Search like normal.** The best thing you can do is to simply browse like normal. If you normally do a couple searches per day, don't try to suddenly start doing 50 random searches to increase your chances of getting paid. This will actually result in you getting paid much less often.

Here are the sites that have paid me to search:

1. **Qmee**
2. **Swagbucks**

3. **Microsoft Rewards**
4. **InstaGC**

**Income potential: 1/5**

# 25.    Get Paid for Your Typing Skills with Data Entry

Can your fingers fly across the keyboard at 60+ words per minute? If so, you can type your way to cash by doing data entry.

The pay is poor, but the faster you can type the better.

**Secret to Success:**

**Accuracy is key** though, so if you make a lot of mistakes you'll have to practice until you can consistently type like a perfectionist.

**Income potential: 2/5**

# 26.    Do Simple Jobs for Amazon with MTurk

Did you know that you can work for Amazon from the comfort of your home?

While **Amazon Mechanical Turk** may not provide the most exciting jobs (data entry, matching stuff, etc.), it can be a great way to earn a little extra spending money.

**Secret to Success:**

**Active users have reported making more than $10,000 per year!**

**Income potential: 3/5**

# 27.    **Play Online Games. Seriously!**

How would you like to play simple, but fun games online…**and get paid for it?**

No, I'm not kidding.

**Swagbucks**, along with several other websites, pay you a couple pennies every time you play one of their simple games.

**Secret to Success:**

This probably won't make you rich, but by the end of the day, you might be able to afford a candy bar. ☐

**Income potential: 1/5**

# 28.　Get Paid to Examine Search Engines

That's right, you can apply to become an evaluator of search engines.

This work is more serious and professional than, say, taking surveys, and some companies will require that you have a degree.

**Secret to Success:**

The pay isn't stellar, but if you have an interest in search engines, this might be a great job for you.

Here are a couple companies that hire search engine evaluators:

- **LionBridge**
- **Appen**

**Income potential: 3/5**

# 29.   **Become an Online Juror**

If you like being a juror, you will love this job.

With **eJury**, you can work from your laptop and participate in mock juries and focus groups via the internet.
**According to ejury.com, eJurors can make $5-$10 depending on the length of the case.**

**Secret to Success:**

You certainly won't get rich, but even one case a week could probably pay for your internet access.

Here are some related sites that pay:

- **JuryTalk**
- **JuryTest**
- **OnlineVerdict**
- **Resolution Research**
- **SignUpDirect**

**Income potential: 2/5**

# 30.    Use Your Ears – Become a Freelance Transcriptionist

Do you think you'd enjoy turning audio into written text?

If so, you may want to look into becoming an online transcriptionist.

The faster you can type, the less time it will take. The less time it takes, the higher your profits!

**Secret to Success:**

**So, if you've got good ears and fast fingers, transcription would be a great part-time job.**

There are a number of websites you can join to find transcription work.

Here's a good start:

- **Rev**
- **Scribie**
- **TranscribeMe**
- **3 Play Media**
- **QuickTate**
- **TigerFish**
- **BabbleType**
- **CastingWords Workshop**
- **CrowdSurf**
- **GoTranscript**
- **SpeechPad**
- **Transcribe.com**
- **ubiQus**
- **SpeakWrite**

**Income potential: 2/5**

# 31.   Sell Your Photos!

As long as you take photos, why not get paid for it?

Even smartphone photography can sell well! Just make sure your photos are of high quality.

Here are a few sites where you can sell your photography:

- **500px**
- **Shutterstock**
- **iStockphoto**
- **Adobe Stock**
- **CanStockPhoto**
- **BigStock**
- **Getty Images**
- **Alamy**
- **Dreamstime**
- **DepositPhotos**
- **123RF**

**Secret to Success:**

**For your smartphone pics, try the Foap app**. You'll get paid $5 every time someone purchases one of your images!

**Income potential: 2/5**

# 32.   Start Investing with These Apps

Looking to become the next Warren Buffett? Okay, stock trading apps probably won't get you there…but they can be a great way to get started!

**Secret to Success:**

There are a number of investment apps out there, but the two that really stand out to me are **Robinhood** and **Acorns**. **Robinhood offers 100% free stock trades**, **and is the only app that does so**.

Plus, there is no minimum balance required to get started.

Robinhood makes its money through Robinhood Gold, which allows users to buy and sell after hours.

**Acorns is a little different: it invests your "spare change".**

So let's say you bought a coffee for $3.60. Acorns will round this up to $4, and invest the remaining $0.40 automatically.

Acorns charges a $1 monthly fee (for accounts with less than $5,000), unless you are a student with a .edu email address – in which case, it's 100% free for four years!

**Income potential: 5/5**

# 33.  Earn Money for Listening to the Radio

Some people like to keep a radio on at all times. Some don't even care what station it's on, just as long as it provides white noise.

**So why not get paid for this?**

**FusionCash** pays you 3 cents every half hour just for listening to the radio. You do have to enter a Captcha code every half hour, but it only takes a second. If you exceed $0.15 in a day, you'll get a $0.01 bonus!

Income potential: 1/5

# 34.   Make Use of Your Eagle Eyes – Become a Freelance Proofreader!

If you find yourself editing in your head while you read, this would be the perfect job for you.

Even the most elite publications oftentimes have typographical and grammatical errors. Nobody's perfect.

**Secret to Success:**

According to the **Editorial Freelancers Association**, proofreaders can expect to earn roughly **$30-35/hour**. Here's a list of sites looking to hire proofreaders (some of them require extensive experience and a college degree):

- **Upwork**
- **Freelancer**
- **Scribbr**

- **Scribendi**
- **Enago**

**Income potential: 4/5**

# 35. Become a Domain Name Flipper

If you're good at coming up with great domain names that aren't already taken, you can purchase them and resell them on **Flippa, Sedo,** or a number of other platforms.

**Secret to Success:**

You can also purchase domains for sale on Flippa or other domain marketplaces, and try to resell them at a markup.

**Desirable domain names can sell for thousands of dollars. Some for hundreds of thousands!**

**Income potential: 5/5**

# 36. Teach People How to Play Chess

Yes, you can get paid for tutoring chess players online through a video call program like Skype.

**And you don't even need to be a grandmaster, or master, for that matter!**

As long as you understand chess very well and are better at it than your student(s), you'll be fine.

**Secret to Success:**

There are several ways to get started:

- Advertise your tutoring service on online chess forums (read the rules first!)
- Offer your service on a website like **SuperProf** or **Care**.

For any online tutoring job, you will need to have a noise-canceling headset.

**Income potential: 3/5**

# 37. Make Money from Your Tweets

If you have a large following on Twitter, this is a great way to rake in the dough.

**Companies will come to you and offer you money in exchange for promoting a product of theirs.**

**Secret to Success:**

The larger a following and the bigger an influence you have, the more you can earn!

**Income potential: 4/5**

# 38. Enter Naming Contests and Unleash Your Creativity

Do you have a knack for coming up with catchy names? Test your skills by entering a naming contest!

When startups just can't come up with a good name themselves, oftentimes they'll turn to the internet for suggestions.

**Secret to Success:**

If you join a naming contest and win, you can earn a hefty prize. **Some contests award more than $500!**
Check out **NamingForce** and **Squadhelp** to get started.

**Income potential: 3/5**

# 39.   Write and Sell Your Very Own eBook

Selling eBooks is one of the oldest and most popular ways to make money online.

Write about a topic you're very knowledgeable about, and then sell it as an eBook for a couple dollars (or more).

You can sell your eBook on a variety of platforms, such as **Amazon** or through **your own website**.

**Secret to Success:**

If you write about popular topics, you can easily make a recurring full-time income.

**Income potential: 5/5**

# 40.   Get Paid to Read Emails (No Joke!)

You likely read emails all the time. What if you could get paid for it?

Believe it or not, you can!

**Secret to Success:**

**Inbox Dollars pays you a few cents for each email you read.**
To get paid, all you have to do is click the link in the email. No need to take any further action after that.

**Income potential: 1/5**

# 41. Add Google AdSense to Your Website

If you have a website, Google AdSense is a great way to monetize it.

Once you sign up, just place the ad code wherever you want, and get paid whenever visitors click an ad!

Google AdSense, and for that matter, any kind of advertising, works best on a site with lots of traffic.

**Secret to Success:**

Only a tiny percentage of visitors click an ad, and since one click is usually worth around a dollar and oftentimes less, **you'll need many thousands of people visiting your site every day in order to generate a healthy income.** Coupled with **affiliate marketing**, Google AdSense can be a great way to turn your website or blog into a lucrative business.

**Income potential: 5/5**

# 42.   Get Paid to Write Product Reviews on Your Website

Many companies are willing to pay bloggers to review certain products.

**Sometimes the payment will be the product itself, sometimes real cash.**

**Secret to Success:**

Before you can expect companies to come knocking on your door, er – email, you'll need to have an established website with lots of loyal visitors.

**Income potential: 3/5**

# 43.   Start Selling Your Products Online with Shopify

Do you have your own products to sell online? One alternative to the likes of Amazon and eBay would be to start your own **Shopify** store.

This means you'll build your own website and sell your products on it.

**Secret to Success:**

You will also be responsible for sending traffic to your site – unlike Amazon, for example, buyers won't find your products unless you promote your site.

There are many ways to get people to your site. Here are some great ones to try:

- **SEO**
- **Social media**
- **Relevant forums**
- **Word of mouth**

Yes, it will take work…but you can quickly become very successful if you work hard enough.

**Income potential: 5/5**

# 44.　Make Big Bucks with Email Marketing

Ever heard the term "the money's in the list"? That refers to an email list.

Email marketing has a huge return on investment, and is an excellent way to drive traffic to your website or your affiliate links.

Before you start, you will want to have a website up and running and a good reason for people to want to join your email list.

Some incentives are as simple as "subscribe to get notified about new blog posts"; some are entire eBooks.

**Secret to Success:**

**The power with having a list is that you own it; you don't have to rely on social media or a platform someone else owns.**
**Income potential: 5/5**

# 45. Start Your Own Patreon Account

Struggling to make an income from your content creation efforts?

**Patreon** could be the answer.

**Secret to Success:**

Especially popular among YouTubers, **Patreon is a great way to accept donations from your fans.**
**Income potential: 4/5**

# 46. Enter and Win Online Slogan Contests

Yes, you can actually get paid pretty well for coming up with clever slogans and taglines.

**Some companies are willing to pay hundreds of dollars for this!**
Finding contests is not difficult.

Just Google "slogan contest" and you'll see lots of good results.

**Secret to Success:**

To get you started, check out the current list of slogan contests on SquadHelp.

Another place to check is **SloganSlingers**.

**Income potential: 3/5**

# 47.   Write Articles for Popular Blogs

If you can write quality, engaging content, you might consider looking into writing for some top blogs.

Your content needs to be unique and meet each website's specific guest-posting guidelines in order to get accepted.

**There are tons of sites that pay for guest posts if you do some digging.**

**Secret to Success:**

**Listverse** currently pays $100 for each accepted submission. You may also want to check out these:

- **A List Apart**
- **International Living**
- **FundsforWriters**
- **Upworthy**

**Income potential: 4/5**

# 48.   Easily Design Your Own T-shirts, Coffee Mugs, and More!

Got an eye for design, or a mind for witty phrases?

You can sell your designs online!

**Cafepress** and **Zazzle** are two examples of websites that print your designs on merchandise. Whenever a product with your design sells, you get a cut!

**Secret to Success:**

You should be aware that unless your designs take off and go viral, you probably won't be able to replace your day job with this.

But hey, anything can happen, right?

Here are some more options (other than Cafepress or Zazzle) to check out:

- **RedBubble**
- **Teespring**
- **society6**
- **Design by Humans**
- **Threadless**
- **SpreadShirt**
- **Pixapp** (phone app)

**Income potential: 4/5**

# 49. Host a Webinar and Share Your Knowledge with the World

Webinars are a great way to share your insights with the world.

**You can make a lot of money from webinars whether they're free to attend, or not!**

Free webinars are far more likely to attract a lot of viewers, so this is what I'd suggest you do.

**Secret to Success:**

You can earn money by directing your viewers to a product you sell, or give them your affiliate link to a product you're promoting. Either way, webinars tend to convert quite well.

Paid webinars probably won't attract as many viewers, but they can still earn you money. Perhaps not as much though.

**Income potential: 4/5**

# 50.  Automatically Save Money with this Free Chrome Extension

**Honey** is a free chrome extension that can save you a lot of money on your online purchases. Time magazine even called it "basically free money".

Honey claims it works on thousands of sites.

**Secret to Success:**

**When you're on the checkout page, click the honey button in your browser extensions and Honey will automatically apply any available coupon codes to your shopping cart.**
**"Income" potential: 2/5**

# 51.   Offer a White Hat Link Building Service

This is for you more advanced people who know SEO.

**Since backlinks are one of Google's top three ranking factors, lots of website owners are more than willing to pay someone to build links to their site.**
Yes, you can offer black-hat (spammy) link-building services on Fiverr for $5…but I would not recommend it. At all.

Instead, if you offer a white-hat link-building service, not only is it ethical, but you can make way more money.

**Secret to Success:**

Genuine white-hat links can be very difficult and time-consuming to build. Therefore, webmasters are willing to shell out a lot of money to outsource the work.

**Income potential: 4/5**

# 52.   Get Paid to do Email Outreach

If you are a great email communicator, you can put your skills to work. Lots of bloggers and businesses are willing to outsource this task.

**Secret to Success:**

The most common type of email outreach is for link-building purposes.

You don't necessarily have to be an SEO or backlink expert to do email outreach though.

As long as you're an effective communicator, you can easily do this.

Income potential: 4/5

# 53.   Join Paribus and Get Refunded for Products that Went Down in Price

**Paribus** is a free app that tracks your online purchases to find price drops, automatically refunding you the difference. In order for it to work, it needs read and write access to your email address, so that it can scan your receipts and compare them with the current price of the product.

**Secret to Success:**

**The trouble is, many people only get a few dollars back even after hundreds of purchases (not necessarily Paribus' fault though).**

"Income" potential: 2/5

# 54.  Sell Your Old Unlimited Data Plan for $1,000

Still got an ancient truly unlimited data plan from the late 2000s?

**You may not realize it, but you're sitting on a goldmine.**

Unlimited data plans are selling for $1,000 on eBay right now.

**Here's why:**

Current unlimited data plans do throttle you down eventually if you use data all the time. But the old unlimited plans, circa 2008-9, are literally unlimited.

**Secret to Success:**

While this may be a bit risky, there is definitely a black market for these unlimited data plans, with people willing to buy them for around one thousand dollars.

# 55.  Build and Sell Ready-Made Niche Websites

For those who love building websites but struggle with growing them, this would be a fantastic option.

**Caution**:
- This is very advanced
- This is not something you can learn in a day
- There's a lot of work involved

With that out of the way, let's proceed.

Ready-made niche sites are very hot these days, and as long as they have several (probably at least 10) pages of unique longform content, **they can sell for over a thousand dollars.**

**Secret to Success:**

For maximum profit, the sites should be aged for at least 6 months, and should have:

- At least 10 pages of longform (1,000+ words) content, and a couple longer pillar articles
- An email optin form with a unique lead magnet (like an eBook)

- A premium theme
- Proper SEO
- The necessary plugins (SEO, security, etc.)
- A logo and branding
- Social media accounts

And as a bonus, offer free skype or email support.

You can either try to sell these websites yourself, or list them on a site like **Flippa**.

**Income potential: 5/5**

# 56.   Design Logos

If designing is your thing, consider designing logos!

Logo designers make about $5 per logo on **Fiverr**, and some even make two logos for that price….

You may also want to check out **48 Hours Logo**, a site that holds logo design contests with cash prizes.

**Secret to Success:**

This won't make you rich, but it's a good side-gig especially if it only takes you a few minutes to come up with a great design.

**Income potential: 3/5**

# 57.   Make Real Money Playing Fantasy Sports

Are you a sports enthusiast? Do you follow professional players and keep track of their stats?

Fantasy sports may be for you – or not. Read on.

You've likely heard about DraftKings and FanDuel, fantasy sports websites through which regular people are supposedly making thousands of dollars.

But the truth is, playing fantasy sports is essentially gambling.

**You build a fantasy team of real players, enter contests, and depending on how well the real players perform, you can make some money or lose it all.**

You see, in order to enter a contest, you have to shell out real cash. And your chances of winning it back are very, very low.

**Secret to Success:**

Pro players use expensive software to analyze player stats, so they're not likely to lose to somebody who manually analyzes stats or goes by their gut.

So, you're actually paying for the low potential to make money. I cannot recommend this and would never try it myself…but if you're willing to take the risk, go for it!

**Income potential: 4/5**

# 58.   Create and Sell Your Own Google Chrome Extensions

Developers only:

Did you know that you can create and sell Chrome extensions? There are several ways to monetize them.

**Secret to Success:**

Google has a **handy guide** for this!

**Income potential: 4/5**

# 59.  Make Money When People Click Your Shortened URLs

Yes, shortening URLs can actually be profitable.

Here's how:

- Shorten a URL with one of the sites linked to below
- Share your new shortened URL on your website, social media, or wherever people will click.
- When someone clicks your URL, they will be shown a short ad before being redirected to the article you shared.

- For every 1,000 views, you'll get paid! Some pay only a few dollars, but others (like Shorte.st) pay up to $15!

**Secret to Success:**

**List of URL shortening sites that pay:**

- **Adf.ly**
- **Shorte.st**
- **Ouo.io**
- **LinkShrink**
- **BC.vc**
- **Oke.io**
- **AdYou.me**
- **Uskip.me**
- **LinkBucks**
- **LinkRex**
- **Fas.li**
- **Short.am**
- **Vivads**
- **Al.ly**

**Income potential: 2/5**

# 60.   Sell Your Email List

If you want to sell your email list, be very careful.

- Most people frown on this.
- Your subscribers probably won't like you anymore
- You can make a lot more money by keeping the list if you know what you're doing.

**But I'm assuming you knew all of the above.**

Email lists are most often paired with a website, product or service. So if you have any of those, sell it along with the list.

**Secret to Success:**

Typically, each subscriber on an email list is valued at $1 (but this depends heavily on a number of factors). **So, a list of 5,000 subscribers is worth approximately $5,000.**

# 61.   Rent Your Email List for Easy Profits

If you want to profit from your email list like never before, consider renting it out to people who want to run solo ads.

**Secret to Success:**

**As long as your email list is sizable, renting it out can easily net you hundreds of dollars.**

If this is the direction you'd like to take, check out **Udimi**.

**Income potential: 3/5**

# 62.   Get Highly Targeted Traffic by Running Solo Ads

Solo ads are a great way to get highly targeted traffic to your landing pages.

Solo Ads or Email Media or Solo Advertising is a way of driving traffic to your landing pages by buying clicks from people with email lists.

**Secret to Success:**

Not all traffic is equal. I have had hundreds of failed campaigns, hundreds of successful campaigns, and I've come to realize that some traffic sources are just not worth it. So choose wisely.

**Income potential: 5/5**

# 63.   Grow a Huge Audience with Social Media Marketing

Social media marketing is one of the best ways to get yourself or your business in front of the masses.

Facebook alone has more active monthly users than the entire country of China.

Twitter has more users than the United States has people.

**Secret to Success:**

Anyone can leverage the power of social media to grow their brand, increase sales, or even get famous. The key is to create content that some group of people would be interested in.

# 64.   **Become a Social Media Manager**

If you are an expert at social media marketing, you have a very valuable skill.

Many businesses are willing to spend a lot of money on social media, and will oftentimes hire experienced social media managers to get the most bang for their buck.

**Secret to Success:**

You can offer your services on a number of platforms, but here are a few good ones to look into:

- **Upwork**
- **CloudPeeps**
- **Fiverr**
- **Indeed**

**Income potential: 4/5**

# 65. Do Online Public Relations

Are you good with public relations?

Google defines public relations as:

"the professional maintenance of a favorable public image by a company or other organization or a famous person."

**Secret to Success:**

There are a lot of public relations jobs to be found online. This isn't a job for newbies, so only get into this line of work if you have experience.

**Upwork** has many public relations jobs available at any given moment.

**Income potential: 4/5**

# 66.    Build Your Own WordPress Plugins or Hire Someone Else to

Can you code? Do you understand WordPress well? You may want to look into creating WordPress plugins. Plugins are basically addons that improve a website's functionality.

**Here are some of the most popular types of plugins:**

- Search Engine Optimization (SEO) enhancements
- Social media sharing buttons
- Membership capabilities
- Insert ads anywhere
- Image optimization=
- Photo galleries

- Contact forms
- Security

**Secret to Success:**

You can make money from your plugin by offering a "pro" version. Be sure to make the pro version worth the cost!

**Income potential: 4/5**

# 67.  Can You Code? Offer Your Services Online!

**Computer programmers are in huge demand these days.** That's because so many people have ideas for applications, programs, and websites, but don't know how to code.

As a good developer, you'll never have a shortage of jobs. Well-paying jobs, to be exact.

**Secret to Success:**

There are a number of places to offer your services, but one of the biggest and most reputable is **Upwork**.

**Income potential: 4/5**

# 68.   Earn a Full-Time Income Designing Websites

Does sitting at your computer all day designing beautiful websites sound appealing?

A web design business can be entirely home-based, and the median salary is quite high – ranging from **$50,000 to $100,000!**

**Secret to Success:**

Use websites like UpWork to gain a following and advertise your services.

**Income potential: 4/5**

# 69.   Know a Second Language? Do Translation Work Online!

If you know more than one language, you have a skill that can easily be monetized!

Many people find themselves in need of a translator – whether they need to translate a document, a website, or even audio. And they're willing to pay for it, too!

**Secret to Success:**

**Translation work certainly won't make you rich – but it could be a great supplemental income stream.**

Here's a list of sites to check out for translation work:

- **Indeed**
- **Translate.com**
- **ProZ**
- **TranslatorsCafe**
- **Gengo**
- **TextMaster**
- **Unbabel**
- **OneHourTranslation**
- **TranslatorsBase**

- **TRADUguide**
- **Lingosaur**

You can also check out Upwork, Fiverr, and other general freelance websites, which will all have plenty of translation jobs available.

**Income potential: 3/5**

# 70.   Start a Podcast in Your Niche

If you haven't noticed already…podcasting is huge! Look at almost every top blog, and you'll see a lot of them have a podcast as well.

That doesn't mean you need a blog in order to start a podcast (although it would help tremendously), **you just need a topic that will fill a gap and that people would actually want to listen to.**

**Secret to Success:**

Pat Flynn is very famous in the podcasting sphere, so if you want to get started, I recommend checking out his course called **Power-Up Podcasting**.

**Income potential: 4/5**

# 71.  Become an Online Newspaper Columnist

This isn't a job that just anyone can do…but if you already have experience as a newspaper columnist, you may be able to find an online newspaper that's willing to hire you.

**Secret to Success:**

The more experience you have, the more money you will be offered.

**Income potential: 4/5**

# 72.  Successfully Start a Viral Blog

If you're constantly staying on top of current trends and news, definitely consider this option.

First, you'll need to **build a website**.
Second, you'll need to create pieces of content (blog posts, videos, etc.) that people will love. For inspiration, check out successful viral websites like Buzzfeed, and model your content after theirs. (Don't ever copy online content – that will get you in big trouble with the search engines, and likely the source!)

Third, you'll need to monetize your website with Google AdSense or an alternative. Place ads in the header, sidebar, and within the blog posts. This is how you'll make money with your site.

Fourth, you'll need to promote your content on social media. If you have the budget, consider running Facebook ads. These aren't too expensive, and will potentially bring you a LOT of visitors.

If you succeeded in creating great content, people will share it like crazy and you just might go viral! **Thousands of visitors per day can easily bring in hundreds of dollars in ad revenue.**

Now, don't get me wrong. Creating a viral website is far more difficult than you probably think. Though these steps may make it sound easy, few people can successfully pull it off. But who knows, maybe you'll be the one to do it. □

**Secret to Success:**

Target a niche that is underserved and growing.

**Income potential: 5/5**

# 73.　**Add Contextual Advertising to Your Website**

Already have a website? You may want to look into monetizing it with contextual ads.

When you sign up with a company like **VigLink**, they will automagically convert certain words on your website into links. These links are affiliate links, and when people click them and purchase a product, **you'll get paid a commission!**

**Secret to Success:**

Literally just sign up to VigLink!

**Income potential: 4/5**

# 74.   Write Content for Revenue Sharing Websites

Are you a good writer but don't have a website? Consider writing for a revenue sharing site like **Hubpages**!

**Secret to Success:**

You'll get paid based on how many people read your article, **so make sure you write content that people like to read** (list posts, shocking news, etc.)

**Income potential: 3/5**

# 75.  Snag Your Piece of the Lucrative CPA Marketing Pie

CPA, or "Cost Per Action" marketing is an online earning method where advertisers pay you whenever a user performs a specific action.

Confusing? Hopefully this will clear it up:

Let's say you find a CPA offer to promote. And let's say this offer is a free insurance quote. You link to the offer from your website. I come along, click your link, and fill out the insurance quote form. Once I hit "submit", you automatically get paid!

Some CPA offers pay simply for a click, some pay for an email, some pay for a form, and some for an actual purchase.

The payouts range widely, but the easy ones (like clicking a link) usually pay out just a few cents, and forms or purchases oftentimes pay as much as $20 (and sometimes more!)

**Secret to Success:**

**As you can see, CPA marketing can be very, very lucrative if you can drive a lot of traffic to your offer.** But, you'll need some guidance on how to do it right before you jump in head first.

Here's a few CPA offer sites to check out as well:

- **MaxBounty**
- **OfferVault**
- **CPALead**
- **ClickBooth**

**Income potential: 5/5**

# 76. **Do Forex Trading**

Like the idea of online investing? You'll want to look into the foreign exchange or "forex". According to **FXCM.com**, the forex market is the largest, most liquid market in the world with an average daily trading volume exceeding $5 trillion.

**That's more than all the world's stock markets…combined!**

**Secret to Success:**

Forex (and investing in general) can be very risky, so if you have no experience, make sure to do a lot of research and/or talk to a financial adviser before you jump in.

**Income potential: 5/5**

# 77.   Test Software for a Full-Time Income

If you're computer-literate and have experience with programming, you could get a job as a software tester.

**Secret to Success:**

**Entry-level software testers can make more than $50,000 per year.**

**Upwork** is a good place to offer your services.

**Income potential: 4/5**

# 78.   Raise Money with a Crowdfunding Campaign

**Crowdfunding is where a large amount of people donate small amounts of money to a certain cause.**

No, you can't start a crowdfunding campaign just to make money (I mean…technically you could)…you will need to convince potential donors that your cause is worthy enough for their support.

**Secret to Success:**

**Kickstarter, Indiegogo, CrowdRise,** and **GoFundMe** are two of the most popular crowdfunding sites, and are used by thousands of people to raise money for businesses, charity, and personal goals.

**Income potential: 5/5**

# 79.   Write Resumes and Cover Letters for other People

Do you have experience writing resumes and cover letters? That's a valuable skill that can earn you some decent cash online.

**Secret to Success:**

Check **Upwork** for these jobs.

**Income potential: 3/5**

# 80.   **Become a Web Hosting Reseller**

**Reseller hosting can be extremely lucrative, but it is a difficult business to break into.** What is it, exactly? Reseller hosting is where you purchase an unlimited hosting plan from companies like Bluehost or GoDaddy, and then resell that hosting to your clients at a markup.

**Secret to Success:**

You can target Shopify businesses with hosting reselling.

**Income potential: 4/5**

# 81.   Get Paid to Promote Companies on Social Media

If you have a social media account with a large (and engaged) following, you may be able to find companies that are willing to pay you to promote their products and brand.

**Secret to Success:**

**You don't want to alienate your followers though, so make sure you only promote brands that are very relevant to your audience.**

**Income potential: 4/5**

# 82.   Self-Publish Your Own Kindle Books

Are you an author? Aspiring or experienced best-seller? Either way, self-publishing your work as a Kindle eBook is a great way to make passive income online.

**Secret to Success:**

Publish under kindle's short reads section to get started

**Income potential: 5/5**

# 83.   Sell Your Videos

Did you know you can sell videos online? That is, as long as they're edited well, and not scrappily done. Here are some websites where you can earn money for your videos:

- **Uscreen**
- **Pond5**
- **Clipcanvas**

**Secret to Success:**

If you happen to capture newsworthy events on camera, you can sell them to major news organizations through **Newsflare**.

**Income potential: 2/5**

# 84.   Become an Internet Life Coach

Life coaches can make a lot of money. If you set up a website and offer your services over the internet, you can get clients from all over the world.

**Secret to Success:**

Hire a coach and see how they do it.

**Income potential: 4/5**

# 85.   Get Paid to Promote Products on Your Website

If your website gets a lot of traffic, chances are companies will be happy to pay you to promote their products to your audience.

**Secret to Success:**

**You can tie this with affiliate marketing to make even more.**

**Income potential: 4/5**

# 86.  Create and Sell Your Own Audiobooks on ACX

Are you an audiobook creator?

You can sell your audiobooks to millions of people through **ACX**. ACX sells audiobooks through Audible and iTunes.

**Secret to Success:**

The voice used should be pleasant to the ear. Have at least one male and one female voice option.

**Income potential: 4/5**

# 87.  Make Money by Answering People's Questions!

You can share your vast knowledge with the world by answering questions!

**Secret to Success:**

There are many Q&A sites that pay users to answer questions. Here are a few of the best:

- **JustAnswer**
- **FixYa**
- **HelpOwl**

The compensation is usually quite low, so don't expect this to replace your income. Even as a side hustle, it's pretty pathetic.

**Income potential: 2/5**

# 88. Create a Profitable Membership Site

If you have a digital product such as an online course, you can create a membership website that requires users to sign up (and pay money) in order to gain access.

**Secret to Success:**

**In the right niche, membership sites can be incredibly lucrative.** However, be aware that it will take a lot of work and time to keep the membership strong and growing. It's definitely not a good option if you're only looking to generate a passive income.

However, it is nonetheless one of the better ways to make a lot of money online.

**Income potential: 5/5**

# 89.   Create a Software, or Hire Someone Else to

**If you know how to develop software, you can easily get into one of the most lucrative sectors of making money online.**

**Secret to Success:**

If you don't know how to code, you can still hire a software developer on **Upwork**. This will require a significant investment, but it can pay off big time in the future.

**Income potential: 5/5**

# 90.   Get Paid to Share Links on Your Social Media Accounts

**ShareMagnet** pays you to share links on social media. Well, sort of. You share links, and when someone clicks that link, you will get paid. You don't get paid if no one clicks the links you share.

I'm not too sure about ShareMagnet's viability for two reasons:

- ShareMagnet's website is rather outdated and there's not much activity
- The payout per link click is pretty low, so you certainly won't get rich.

**Secret to Success:**

I'll let you decide for yourself.

**Income potential: 1/5**

# 91. Earn an Extra $159/Year in Passive Income with Cross Media Panel

**If you're not too concerned about privacy, you can earn an extra $159/year passively with Cross Media Panel.** If you connect three devices, you are compensated with $6, and then $3 per week thereafter. Not bad for virtually no work!

**Secret to Success:**

You can join Cross Media Panel instantly

**Income potential: 2/5**

# 92. Get Paid to Play Mobile Games

If you like to play mobile games, you'll be happy to know you can get paid for it!

**AppKarma pays you to try out different games**. If you are an active user (1 hour/day), you can earn about $14 per month – or $168 a year!

You can also earn by referring others to AppKarma. You'll earn 30% of what your referrals make for life (at no expense to your referrals)!

**Secret to Success:**

When you join AppKarma and enter a referral code, you'll get 300 points!

**Income potential: 2/5**

# 93.   **Review Phone Calls**

Good listeners wanted! Humanatic is a company that pays you to listen to phone calls and then categorize them.

The pay is fairly low at several cents per call, but as you gain experience and improve your accuracy, your pay will go up.

**Secret to Success:**

**You can cash out your earnings to PayPal every Monday as long as you have accumulated at least $10.**

If you think this is worth the time, you can join Humanatic.

**Income potential: 2/5**

# 94.　Get Paid to Listen to Music

Are you a music fanatic?

**SliceThePie** pays its users to review music. Each review needs to be about 50-100 words, and cannot be fake (they scan reviews and reject them if they don't seem legitimate).

**For your trouble, they'll pay you a few pennies**.

Yes, that means you'll have to review several hundred songs in order to earn just $10.

**Secret to Success:**

You can also earn money via their referral program. You'll make 10% of what your referrals make, which is low for these types of sites.

You may also want to check out **Musicxray**, which is similar to SliceThePie.

## 95. Get Paid to Comment on Forums

If you have an excellent handle on grammar and the English language, you could get paid to comment on forums.

This won't earn you a full-time income, but it could certainly pay your internet bill.

**Secret to Success:**

Check out **Paid Forum Posting** or forum posting jobs available on **Upwork**.

Income potential: 2/5

## 96. Make Money in College – Sell Your Class Notes!

**How would you like to earn an extra $1,000 per month while in college?**

It doesn't even require much work if you already take thorough notes!

There are many sites that allow you to upload your notes and get paid every time someone purchases them. Since they are digital, you can sell an unlimited number of the same note! Check out these sites to get started:

- **StudySoup**
- **StudentVIP**
- **OneClass**
- **Stuvia**
- **NotesGen**
- **Nexus Notes**

**Secret to Success:**

Hint: the best way to make a lot of money selling your classnotes is by word of mouth. Tell your classmates about the notes and study guides you have for sale, and if they are serious about earning a good grade, they'll likely buy!

**Income potential: 3/5**

# 97.  Sell Literally Anything on eBay

**eBay** has been around since 1995, and remains one of the top marketplaces on the internet.

You can sell anything on eBay. ANYTHING.

You can choose to sell an item as an auction, or as a "buy it now". Auctions usually get more views and activity, but don't always go as high as you'd like. So if you KNOW the worth of your item, list it as a buy it now (or put a reserve on the auction).

**Note that being an eBay seller does require some work. You have to manage inventory, paperwork, and the shipping of your sold items. It's not too difficult though.**

**Secret to Success:**

How profitable you can be on eBay depends entirely on what you have for sale. Some sellers only make a few dollars, and others make millions per year.

Income potential: 5/5

## 98.  Make a Killing Selling on Amazon

Amazon is the largest marketplace on the web. So, naturally, you can make a lot of money as an Amazon seller.

There is a variety of ways to earn money with Amazon. You can sell your own products directly on Amazon, do Amazon FBA, or even join the Amazon Associates (affiliate) program and never have to worry about inventory.

**Secret to Success:**

**All three options require a lot of hard work and patience, but they are all among the most lucrative ways to make money online.**
**Income potential: 5/5**

## 99.  Sell Your Handmade and Vintage Items on Etsy

**Etsy** is the marketplace of choice for selling handcrafted and vintage items. If you enjoy making things by hand, you should look into becoming an Etsy seller.

**Secret to Success:**

Handmade is all the rage, so a lot of Etsy sellers are easily earning a full-time income.

**Income potential: 5/5**

# 100. Make Money Clipping Coupons

Everyone knows coupons are a great way to save money, but did you know they can be a great way to MAKE money as well?

**In fact, there are a couple ways to make money clipping coupons:**

- Clip all the coupons you can find from cereal boxes, magazines, newspapers, etc. Search for online coupon sites, and print out all the coupons you can.

Once you have a pile of coupons, **start listing them on eBay!**

**Secret to Success:**

**Tip**: See what similar coupons are selling for, and price yours accordingly.

- Print coupons off of Swagbucks and Inbox Dollars! Not only will you save money with these coupons, **you will also earn about 10 cents for every coupon you redeem!**

**Income potential: 2/5**

# 101.  Sell Your Teaching Materials on TeachersPayTeachers

Are you a teacher? There's money to be made!

**Secret to Success:**

You can sell lesson plans, printables, and more at **TeachersPayTeachers**.

In most cases, this provides a decent supplementary income, although some teachers are making as much as a full-time income.

**Income potential: 3/5**

# 102.  Rent Your Untouched Clothes Online

If you have clothes that never get worn, consider renting them to strangers online!

**Some people make $1,000 per month doing this.**
**Secret to Success:**

To get started, check out **Stylelend** and the **RentMyWardrobe** app.
**Income potential: 3/5**

# 103.  Rent Out Your Bike, Surfboard or Snowboard

# Online and Make Up to $500/Month

Do you have extra gear lying around, say, bicycles, surfboards, or snowboards?

**Secret to Success:**

You can rent those to strangers with **SpinLister** and make up to $500/month!

**Income potential: 3/5**

## 104.  Sell Your Old Cell Phones and Electronics

Have any electronics just sitting around, no longer getting used? You could trade them in for real cash!

There are several sites you should check out if you want to do this:

- **Gazelle**
- **Decluttr**
- **Orchard**

- **Swappa**
- **Glyde**

**Secret to Success:**

Another option is to sell your electronics on **eBay**. Though the process is a little more involved, you may be able to get a little bit more for your device.

# 105. Sell Books Online for Cash

If you have any books sitting around that you aren't going to read, you might as well cash them in!

**Secret to Success:**

See what your books are worth with **BookFinder**, and sell them for the highest offer!

# 106. Get Paid to Scan Your Shopping Receipts

Nielson ratings is most commonly known as the company that pays families to take surveys about TV and radio.

But now they offer something new: **Nielson Homescan**. After you sign up, they'll send you a free scanner. Every time you go shopping, you simply scan the barcodes on the back of each product and send your data off to Nielsen.

**Secret to Success:**

As an active participant, you'll receive points that go toward gift cards and free sweepstake entries.

**Prizes include money, vacations, and even brand-new vehicles.**

# 107.  **Turn Junk You Find on the Curb into Cash**

Looking to earn a little extra cash on the side?

**Secret to Success:**

**Pick up the junk you find on the curb and list it on the LetGo app!**

# 108. Get Free Money from Class-Action Settlements

There could be free money waiting for you.

**Secret to Success:**

The Penny Hoarder has an **ongoing list** of class-action settlements that could potentially net you **thousands of dollars.**

# 109. Sell Sports and Concert Tickets Online

If you have extra event tickets just lying around, you might as well turn them into cash!

**Secret to Success:**

**StubHub** is the largest marketplace for event tickets.

# 110.   Find Virtual Odd-Jobs on TaskRabbit

**TaskRabbit** is an app that pays you to run errands for other people. Most errands require you to actually get off your computer, drive or walk to a nearby store, purchase a few items, and deliver them.

**Secret to Success:**

There are some virtual tasks as well. If you only want to make money online, keep a look out for these jobs.

**Income potential: 2/5**

# 111.   Turn Old Newspapers and Magazines into Cash

Got any old newspapers or magazines lying around?

They should be about 30 or more years old, and the older the better.

**What you do is cut out the ads, and sell them on eBay. Buy frames for the ads from the dollar store, and you can charge even more.**

**Secret to Success:**

The more eye-catching the ad, the more it can sell for. Most sell for about $5, but some go for a whole lot more.

**Income potential: 3/5**

# 112.  **Sell Stuff Locally on Craigslist**

If you want to sell items that may be difficult to pack and ship, you can sell them on **Craigslist**.

Local buyers turn to Craigslist for things like couches, pianos, vehicles, and other large items. Even animals can find new homes via Craigslist.

**Secret to Success:**

When someone purchases your item (or animal), you'll give them your address and they will pick it up in person.

# 113. List Your Items for Sale on the Facebook Marketplace

The **Facebook Marketplace** is a good alternative to Craigslist.

**Secret to Success:**

It basically works the same as Craigslist, except it'll be people on Facebook that will see your ads.

# 114. Get Paid Real Money for Your Junk Mail

"Wait! Don't throw that away!"

**You can actually earn money for your junk mail – both physical mail and emails!**

**SBK Center** pays you to send them your junk mail. They use the junk mail for market research.

You can't expect to get rich doing this. In fact, you'll probably earn about **$20 every 10 weeks**. But that's not too bad if you think about it.

**Secret to Success:**

Selling your junk mail could increase your holiday spending budget by more than $100!

**Income potential: 2/5**

# 115. Turn Your Talents into Cash with Online Competitions

Is there something you are particularly good at? If it's something that can be done online, chances are there are contests you can enter.

**Secret to Success:**

**Prizes will of course vary depending on the contest.** This may not be the best way to earn a sustainable income, but if you are really good at what you do it could definitely help.

# 116. Win Free Stuff with Online Sweepstakes

This option may not be for everyone, but there are plenty of legit sweepstakes you can enter online if you know where to look.

Different companies are running sweepstakes all the time, so a good place to look is on social media.

You can also search for sweepstakes on sweepstake directories.

**Secret to Success:**

Though this is technically a way to make money online, it's not reliable nor sustainable. Not by a long shot.

But, there's always the chance that it could turn out to be a profitable way to spend 5 minutes doing each morning.

# 117.  Sell Your Digital Product on Clickbank

Have you created a digital product, such as an eBook or an online course? One of the best ways to sell it is through affiliate sites like **Clickbank**.

**Secret to Success:**

**Using this method, you won't have to do any of the promotion yourself.** Clickbank affiliates will find your product, and trust me, they will do plenty of promotion. That's because the affiliates get a small cut for each sale. So, make sure to take this into account when pricing your product.

You want it to be affordable, but you also want to make sure it's worth the affiliates' time to promote it!

**Income potential: 5/5**

# 118. Help People Solve Problems as an Online Consultant

Do you have extensive knowledge in a specific field?

One of the most profitable ways to turn that knowledge into cash is by offering a consulting service.

**As a consultant or teacher, you'll be mentoring and helping your students solve problems they are facing.**

**Secret to Success:**

There are several online consultant sites such as **Clarity**, **Coach.me**, and **Savvy**, but you can also offer consulting services on your own site, or on LinkedIn.

**Income potential: 4/5**

# 119.  Find Unclaimed Money You are Owed

**Did you know that right now, as you're reading this, the state might owe you a pretty penny?**

In fact, there are billions of dollars of unclaimed money in the United States alone.

This money comes from a variety of sources, such as life insurance policies, inactive bank accounts, uncashed checks, unclaimed trust distributions, unclaimed refunds of mortgage insurance, forgotten retirement accounts, and more.

**Let's be realistic though:**

Chances are slim that you have unclaimed money. Still, the possibility is there, so why not take a few minutes to check?

**Secret to Success:**

You can search for unclaimed money for free on **Unclaimed.org**. Click your state (or province or country), and it will take you to a page where you can start the process of locating any possible unclaimed cash.

# 120.  Cook Your Way to Cash with Online Recipe Contests

If you are a culinary genius, you can make money online!

At any given time, there are plenty of online **recipe contests** that you can enter. Some offer as much a $5,000 for first place!

**Secret to Success:**

Just be sure to read all the rules beforehand. But other than that, simply put on your chef's cap and work your magic!

**Income potential: 3/5**

# 121.  **Sell Your Music**

Want to make money selling your beats? Well, you're in luck!

**CDBaby**, **TuneCore**, and **ReverbNation** are three sites that distribute your music to major platforms. I'm talking iTunes, Spotify, Pandora, Amazon Music, Google Play, Deezer, and more.

**Secret to Success:**

As long as your music is actually good, **these sites will give a tremendous kickstart to your music career**.

**Income potential: 5/5**

# 122. Sell Your Art Online

No need to be the starving artist.

**Secret to Success:**

ArtsyShark **has a list** of more than 250 places to sell art online!

**Income potential: 5/5**

# 123. Charge People to Place Ads on Your Website

Do you have a lot of traffic coming to your website? If so, you might consider monetizing portions of your sidebar(s), header, or footer by allowing people to place an ad in one of these spots for a fee.

**Secret to Success:**

To get started, you could have a "Your Ad Here" block in your sidebar which, when clicked, takes the user to a page explaining your advertising guidelines and encouraging them to fill out the required form.

## 124. Earn a Stable Income as a Call Center Representative

For people who enjoy talking on the phone, working from home as a call center representative is a good option for earning a stable income.

**Secret to Success:**

Check out these sites if you want to go down this path:

- **Arise**
- **Working Solutions**

**Income potential: 3/5**

## 125. Make Six Figures as a Blog Manager

If you are very experienced with all aspects of blogging, you have a valuable skill that many companies will pay for. **In fact, some companies will pay as much as six figures for a blog manager!**

As a blog manager, you'll be writing posts, scheduling posts, posting to social media, managing SEO, and perhaps even managing a team of writers.

**Secret to Success:**

A good way to get a job as a blog manager is to create press kit, and introduce yourself to companies, letting them know you are interested in a job as a blog manager.

**Income potential: 4/5**

# 126. Earn a Massive Income with Search Engine Optimization

Search engine optimization is the art of ranking websites high in the search engines results.

**You can make money with SEO by getting your own money-making websites to rank high, or by offering to do SEO for another company.**

**Secret to Success:**

If you are exceptional at SEO, you can charge a lot of money for your services. Otherwise, you'll have to prove yourself on platforms like Upwork and Fiverr.

**Income potential: 5/5**

# 127. Make Money Online as a Voice Over Artist

If you have a good, clear voice, you could offer a voice over service on **Fiverr**.

You could charge different amounts based on factors such as length, content, and delivery time. See what other successful voice over artists are doing, and model your service after theirs. Add a unique twist to it to really stand out.

**Secret to Success:**

You will have a lot of competitors since voice overs are one of Fiverr's main categories, so you will definitely have to do some marketing on social media, your website, or by word of mouth.

**Income potential: 4/5**

## 128.  Need a Quick $1,000? Read a "How-to" Article and Offer the Process as a Service

**This is probably the best way to legitimately earn a quick $1,000 online.**

What you do is read a detailed "how-to" article, and offer a service implementing the practices you learned in that article.

For example, you could read a detailed guide about "Guestographic link building", and then approach bloggers and pitch them with a document explaining your service.

In the document, you can list everything offered in your service, as well as the price – which you can charge more for the more valuable your service is.

It requires:

- NO money
- NO website
- NO business card

**Secret to Success:**

This may sound sort of confusing, so I recommend you read the article "How to make $1000 dollars in the next 14 days without an idea" by Brian Harris, on the VideoFruit website.

# 129. Become an Online Mystery Shopper

Mystery shopping is where you pretend to be a real customer, but really, you're secretly gathering information about the company – such as how you were treated.

**Secret to Success:**

Although most mystery shopping jobs require you to actually visit physical stores, **there are a few online mystery shopping jobs which are mostly phone-based.**
Pay varies depending on the job, but usually you'll get at least $10 per job, and a reimbursement on any purchases you made.

**Income potential: 2/5**

# 130. **Do in-depth Research for Other People**

If you can perform detailed and in-depth research, you may be a great candidate for a job at **AskWonder**.
Your job will be to answer questions – most of them very difficult, even with extensive research.

**Secret to Success:**

The pay is quite low, and for most people it's below minimum wage. However, this is far better than doing surveys all day, although the latter would take less thought.

# 131. Invest in Crypto currency for a Potentially Massive Profit

Crypto currencies like Bitcoin and Ethereum are all the rage these days, and for good reason. **They're basically like a modern-day gold rush!**

As with any kind of investment, investing in crypto currencies is certainly risky – especially since a lot of people believe "the bubble" is about to burst.

However, it's also how a lot of people **turned several thousand dollars into several million in just a few years**. If you don't mind taking risks, investing in crypto currencies may end up being one of the smartest risks you've taken.

**Secret to Success:**

Before you get started, make sure to do a lot of research. This isn't something you can just start doing thoughtlessly.

You will thank yourself many times over if you take the time it requires to thoroughly research before you begin.

Investing in a crypto currency will cost money – nobody's giving away free bitcoins. However, at the rate things are going, it's not impossible to make back your investment in a matter of days….

**Income potential: 5/5**

# 132. Keep Clients Informed of the Latest News in their Industry

Many people need to keep up with the latest news in their industry, which takes up a lot of their time. **If you could offer a news clipping service, it would save them time and earn you a quick buck.**

As a news clipper, you would be doing all the research for them, weeding out any news that's not worthwhile. At the end of the day, or at a specific time interval, you would send them all the worthwhile news.

**Secret to Success:**

It may be a bit difficult to find a job as a news clipper, but probably the best way to find employment would be to go to different networking events and pitch your service during conversations.

**Income potential: 2/5**

# 133. Create and Sell WordPress Themes

If you can code and are familiar with WordPress, creating themes can be a great way to earn money online.

**Even if you can't code, you can hire a developer on Upwork or a similar site to develop themes for you.** Yes, this will have an upfront cost, but it could potentially pay off big time if you create truly great themes.

**Secret to Success:**

Themes should be responsive, secure, SEO optimized, and follow the **WordPress coding standards**. And they should look awesome, too.

**Income potential: 5/5**

# 134. Charge People to Add Links to Your Directory

If you can create a popular business directory within a specific niche, you could charge businesses a fee if they want to get added to your directory.

**Secret to Success:**

You will have to get a LOT of traffic before you can charge anything worthwhile, since there are so many other routes businesses can take to market themselves. In other words, **you'll have to make sure getting listed in your directory is worth the cost.**

# 135. Be a Professional Gamer

Are you a skillful player of any popular online games?

**Secret to Success:**

If so, there are several routes you can take to earn money with your passion:

- **Start a YouTube channel** – record videos of yourself playing, and earn revenue from the ads. Some of the top YouTubers in the world are gamers.
- **Play professionally** – many games have leagues and tournaments, and some of them offer cash prizes to the winners.

**Income potential: 5/5**

# 136. Make Money Uploading, Downloading, and Sharing Files

There are a number of popular Pay Per Download (PPD) websites, which pay you a few cents each time someone downloads your file.

**What you do is upload your file to one of these websites, and then share the download link on your own website or with your social media followers. When someone downloads your file, you'll be paid!**

**Secret to Success:**

Make sure to do a lot of research before getting started with PPD. **This industry is rife with scams, so be aware of that when making any decisions!**

**Income potential: 2/5**

# 137. Earn Money by Clicking Ads

Clicking ads on a Paid To Click or "PTC" website is definitely the easiest way to earn a few cents with no monetary investment.

You can literally join a PTC site, and start clicking ads. Each ad click is usually worth a fraction of a cent, rarely more.

**Secret to Success:**

A while back, I signed up with one of the largest PTC sites, **Clixsense**, and spent about two hours clicking ads. **In the end, I had amassed $0.07! (not a typo).** The reason I stopped (aside from the fact that it was a huge waste of time) was that there were no more ads to click!

Granted, there are other ways to make money on a PTC site – such as completing offers, and getting referrals. But neither of those options are worth the time when you consider how much more you could earn with other make money online opportunities.

**Income potential: 1/5**

# 138. **Report Bugs on Major Websites and Earn Up to $31,337**

Many major websites, such as **Google** and **Facebook**, have bug bounty programs. The reward for finding a bug can range anywhere from several hundred, to tens of thousands of dollars.

**Secret to Success:**

**Google's top reward is $31,337 – a full salary for some.**

# 139. **Write Guest Posts on Major Sites for Clients**

If you enjoy writing and are good at it, you may want to look into ghost-writing guest posts for other people.

Guest posting is a powerful SEO tactic, but many people find it time consuming and would rather hire someone else to do it for them.

**Secret to Success:**

**If your content is high quality, you can expect to earn a decent income doing this**. A lot of content creators charge 5 to 10 cents per word, but charge what you believe your writing is worth.

**Income potential: 4/5**

# 140. **Invest in Online Businesses**

If you already have a good amount of cash on hand, you might consider investing in online businesses through **CrowdCube** or a similar investing website.

**Secret to Success:**

As with any kind of investing, there are a lot of risks involved. Still, a lot of online businesses take off and become very profitable for investors. Just make sure you understand what you're getting yourself into before you jump in.

**Income potential: 5/5**

# 141.  Start Your Own Forum

If you are passionate about a particular subject, you might want to look into building a forum where you can bring together a community of like-minded individuals.

**Secret to Success:**

**Forums with a lot of traffic can make a decent amount of money through ads and affiliate links.**
One downside to starting a forum is that unless you have a ready and waiting audience, forums are extremely difficult to grow. And that is especially true if you are just starting out, with little to no experience. Don't ask how I know, haha.

**Income potential: 5/5**

# 142. Earn Real Crypto Cash for Being Active on Steemit

**Steemit** is a new social media website that's seeing explosive growth. Probably because users can earn real money, in the form of "Steem" coins.

On the front page, you'll see a list of the top blog posts, and it even shows how much money those posts have generated (sometimes in the thousand-dollar range).

**Secret to Success:**

Definitely worth checking out if you're remotely interested in the crypto currency space!

**Income potential: 4/5**

# 143. Make Money Selling Your Unwanted Gift Cards

If you have any gift cards lying around that you'll never use, why don't you sell them on **eBay**? There are bound to be many interested buyers.

You'll probably have to sell them at a discount, so for example, a $20 gift card may only go for $15. It really depends on what company the gift card is for.

**Secret to Success:**

Oddly enough, I saw some $20 gift cards going for a lot more than $20 (like really??) so yeah, the prices people will pay are all over the map.

# 144. Join Medium's Partner Program and Make Money from Your Posts

Medium is a social network for writers. People can post their articles on Medium, grow a following, and now, make money!

**Secret to Success:**

If you write awesome content and have a large following, you could turn this into a good side-hustle or even a full-time income. In fact, Medium reports that the highest-earning author in January 2018 earned a total of **$11,316.74** for the month!

You can read more about Medium's Partner Program **here**.

**Income potential: 4/5**

# 145.  Get Paid Bitcoin Cash for Using Yours.org!

**Yours** is a fairly new social network, but that doesn't mean it should be ignored. You seriously might regret it if you ignored it, in fact.

Here's why:

Unlike Facebook, or Twitter, or basically every other social network, you can actually get paid for using Yours.

You get paid in **Bitcoin Cash** when people vote or comment on your posts, tip you, or purchase your content. Yes, you read that right. You can hide a portion of your post behind a paywall, and charge people whatever you want in order for them to access the hidden content.

You can even earn money for voting other people's posts. According to their **FAQ** page;

Each vote costs 25¢ and the payment goes to earlier voters and the creator. If many people vote on the same content after you, you profit.

For example, suppose Alice makes a post. Bob votes on her post and pays 25¢ to Alice. Then Carol votes on the post and pays 25¢: 12.5¢ goes to Alice and 12.5¢ goes to Bob. Then Dave votes on the post and pays 25¢: 8.3¢ goes to Alice, 8.3¢ goes to Bob, and 8.3¢ goes to Carol. The first quarter of voters always profit.

I made over $6 in the first couple of days as a member, and that was only from one post that took me a few minutes to write.

The potential is huge.

**Secret to Success:**

To get started, you'll want to sign up on **Yours**, click "deposit", and then sign up with **Coinbase** and purchase around $5 of Bitcoin Cash. Once that's all done, you should be good to go!

**Income potential: 4/5**

# 146. This is How to Get Products for Free

Do you like getting free products? Who doesn't, right?

**BzzAgent is a website that sends you products for free.** You then have to try them out, tell your friends about them, and write a Bzz report on the product.
After that, you can keep the product forever.

**Secret to Success:**

Unfortunately, to become a Bzz agent, you have to fill out a lot of forms which ask for very personal information – such as your medical history, family tree information, and pretty much everything except your social security number. That right there is a deal breaker for most people. So if you can tough it out, you will succeed.

# 147.  Make Hundreds in Passive Income by Using Your Car as Ad Space

If you don't mind having an advertisement on your car, you could make an extra $100 or more per month.

There are several companies that pay you to wrap your car in an ad.

**Wrapify pays by the mile, with some drivers making $400-$600 per month.**
**Carvertise pays monthly, usually at a rate of $100, but sometimes up to $200.**
Both will require you to do a lot of driving in high-traffic locations. Don't expect to get accepted if you live out in the middle of nowhere, or don't drive very often.

The wraps are put on by the company for a set period of time. Don't worry, the wraps will not harm your vehicle – in fact, they protect the paint! When your campaign ends, the company will remove the wrap.

**Secret to Success:**

Unlike the many car wrapping scams out there, neither of the two companies I listed require an upfront payment. It's absolutely free to do, and is a great way to earn some extra passive income.

# 148.  **Rent Out Your Driveway**

Do you live in a metropolitan area, and have an empty driveway? You could make hundreds of dollars per month!

There are a number of apps where you can list your parking space, name your price and the availability, and get paid whenever someone rents the space.

The pay varies considerably based on where you live. **In San Francisco for example, you could make as much as $19 per day. In the Boston suburbs on the other hand, you could expect about $2.75.**

Note that renting out a parking space is not legal in every jurisdiction. Portland, Oregon is one place where it's not allowed. So, make sure it's legal in your area before you try it!

**Secret to Success:**

Here are a few parking apps/websites to try out:

- **Spot app**
- **JustPark**
- **MonkeyParking**

# 149. **Rent Out Your Spare Room with Airbnb**

Want to make money from your spare room, or your entire villa? Now you can with **Airbnb**!

Some people think it's creepy hosting strangers in their accommodations, but others don't mind the idea – especially if they're fairly compensated.

With Airbnb, you can take pictures of your room, put up a listing, and if someone is passing through your area and needs somewhere to stay, they can book your room for a fee.

Obviously, Airbnb is most effective in densely populated areas. But even if you're in a smaller town, you may still get the occasional booking.

**Secret to Success:**

**You can also host "Experiences" on Airbnb. Some examples include culture walks, learning to cook a new dish, and photography classes.**
After spending a little time exploring Airbnb, you'll see just how creative you can get.

Well, I guess that concludes the world's most comprehensive list of ways to make money online. I hope you were able to find your dream internet job, or at least some inspiration!

# 150. Sell a to a Specialty Market

Want to make money from your home without any additional supplies?

**Secret to Success:**

There are people who would pay substantially for tears, fingernail clippings and other weird items online.

www.ingramcontent.com/pod-product-compliance
Lightning Source LLC
Chambersburg PA
CBHW030649220526
45463CB00005B/1696